W9-CUD-191

U.S.A. TRAVEL GUIDES

IOWA

BY ANN HEINRICHS • ILLUSTRATED BY MATT KANIA

The Child's World®
childsworld.com

Published by The Child's World®
1980 Lookout Drive • Mankato, MN 56003-1705
800-599-READ • www.childsworld.com

Photo Credits
Photographs ©: Ron Thomas/iStockphoto, cover, 1;
Phil Roeder CC2.0, 7; regan76 CC2.0, 8, 23; Gabriela
Dolezelova/Shutterstock Images, 11; Cheri Lord/The
Ottumwa Courier/AP Images, 12; National Park Service,
15; Photographs in the Carol M. Highsmith Archive/
Library of Congress, 16, 20, 32; Andre Jenny Stock
Connection Worldwide/Newscom, 19; Nancy Nehring/
iStockphoto, 24; Joseph Sohm/Shutterstock Images,
27; Matthew Putney/Waterloo Courier/AP Images, 28;
iStockphoto, 31; Denise Krebs CC2.0, 35; Shutterstock
Images, 37 (top), 37 (bottom)

ISBN 9781503819559
LCCN 2016961131

Printing
Printed in the United States of America
PA02334

Ann Heinrichs is the author of more than 100 books for children and young adults. She has also enjoyed successful careers as a children's book editor and an advertising copywriter. Ann grew up in Fort Smith, Arkansas, and lives in Chicago, Illinois.

About the Author
Ann Heinrichs

Matt Kania loves maps and, as a kid, dreamed of making them. In school he studied geography and cartography, and today he makes maps for a living. Matt's favorite thing about drawing maps is learning about the places they represent. Many of the maps he has created can be found in books, magazines, videos, Web sites, and public places.

About the
Map Illustrator
Matt Kania

On the cover: Iowa produced more than 2.5 billion bushels (88.1 million cubic m) of corn in 2015.

OUR IOWA TRIP

Shall we take a trip through Iowa today? You'll find it's a great place to explore. Here's just a taste of what's to come.

You'll ride your bike through the countryside. You'll watch wildlife and explore caves. You'll see huge earthen mounds shaped like animals. You'll gaze upon miles of leafy cornfields. You'll learn about old-time farm life. You'll watch windmills on a wind farm. You'll see how tractors and ice cream are made. And you'll meet some champion hogs!

Are you ready to roll? Then buckle up and hang on tight. We're off to discover Iowa!

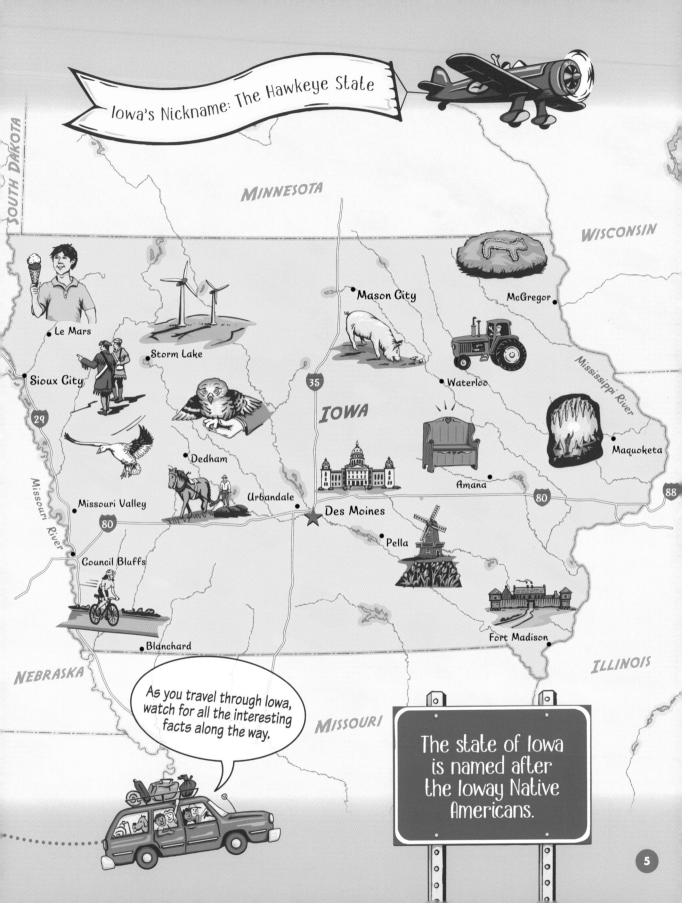

Iowa's Nickname: The Hawkeye State

SOUTH DAKOTA

MINNESOTA

WISCONSIN

Le Mars

Storm Lake

Sioux City

29

IOWA

Mason City

McGregor

Waterloo

Mississippi River

Dedham

Maquoketa

Missouri Valley

Urbandale

Amana

80

88

80

Des Moines

Council Bluffs

Pella

Missouri River

Blanchard

Fort Madison

NEBRASKA

ILLINOIS

As you travel through Iowa, watch for all the interesting facts along the way.

MISSOURI

The state of Iowa is named after the Ioway Native Americans.

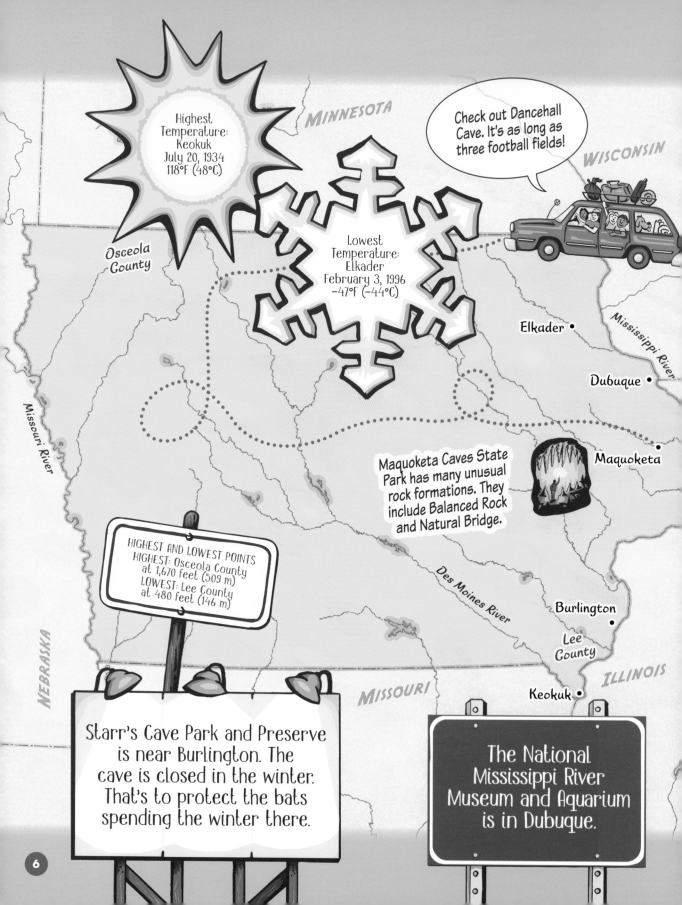

Highest Temperature:
Keokuk
July 20, 1934
118°F (48°C)

Check out Dancehall Cave. It's as long as three football fields!

Lowest Temperature:
Elkader
February 3, 1996
–47°F (–44°C)

Maquoketa Caves State Park has many unusual rock formations. They include Balanced Rock and Natural Bridge.

HIGHEST AND LOWEST POINTS
HIGHEST: Osceola County at 1,670 feet (509 m)
LOWEST: Lee County at 480 feet (146 m)

Starr's Cave Park and Preserve is near Burlington. The cave is closed in the winter. That's to protect the bats spending the winter there.

The National Mississippi River Museum and Aquarium is in Dubuque.

MINNESOTA
WISCONSIN
Osceola County
Elkader
Mississippi River
Dubuque
Maquoketa
Missouri River
Des Moines River
Burlington
Lee County
NEBRASKA
MISSOURI
ILLINOIS
Keokuk

MAQUOKETA CAVES STATE PARK

W ander through Dancehall Cave or Dugout Cave. Glistening rock formations are everywhere. You're exploring Maquoketa Caves State Park! It's in eastern Iowa near Maquoketa.

Prairies and rolling hills cover most of Iowa. The state lies between two big rivers. The Mississippi River forms the eastern border. Cliffs and rugged hills rise in the northeast.

The Missouri River outlines most of the western border. Tall **bluffs** overlook this river. The Des Moines River cuts through central Iowa. It flows from northwest to southeast. Then it enters the Mississippi River at Keokuk.

Explore Dancehall Cave at Maquoketa Caves State Park!

BIKING THE WABASH TRACE NATURE TRAIL

Do you like bike riding? Try biking the Wabash Trace Nature Trail. It stretches from Council Bluffs to Blanchard. You bike along steep, sharply curving hills. You pass farms and villages. And you wind through leafy forests. Tree branches seem to form a shelter around you. You feel like you're in a green tunnel!

Biking is a favorite outdoor activity in Iowa. It's one of many ways to enjoy nature. Camping, boating, fishing, and swimming are popular, too. Some people like hiking in northeastern Iowa. Climbing those rugged hills is quite a workout!

Enjoy the trees along the Wabash Trace Nature Trail in autumn.

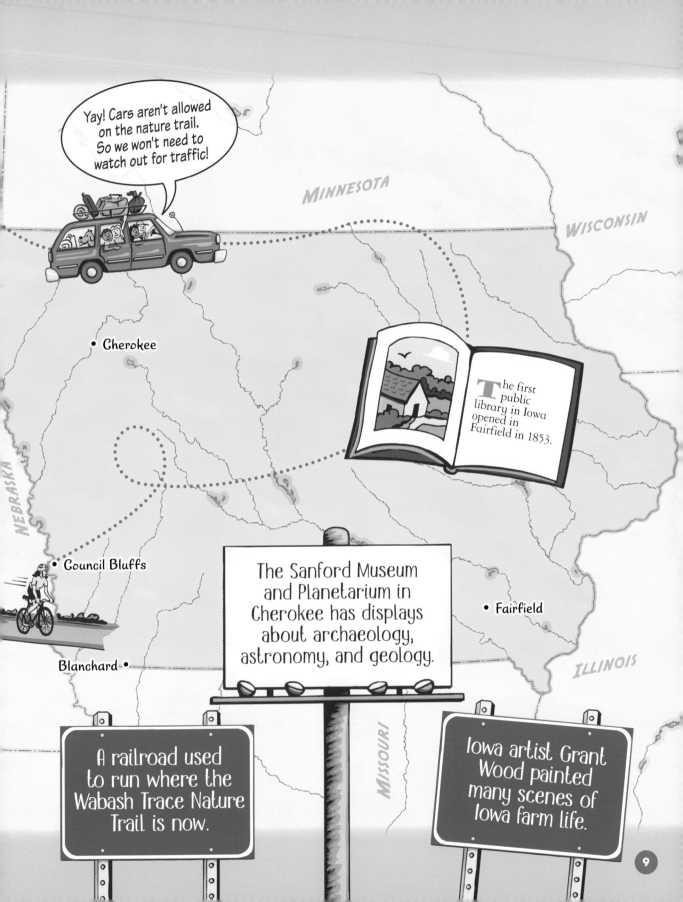

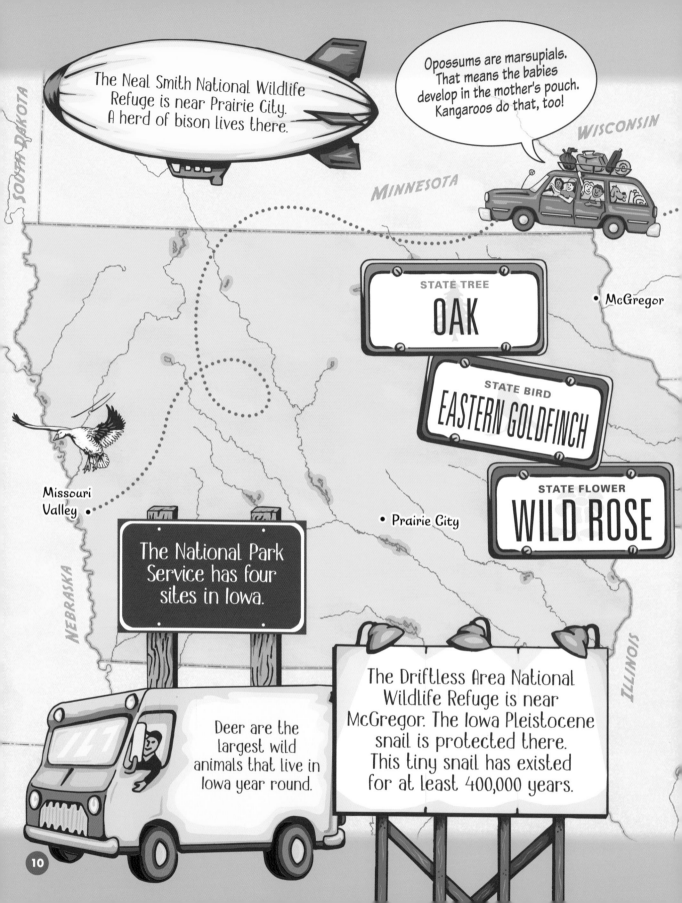

The Neal Smith National Wildlife Refuge is near Prairie City. A herd of bison lives there.

Opossums are marsupials. That means the babies develop in the mother's pouch. Kangaroos do that, too!

STATE TREE
OAK

STATE BIRD
EASTERN GOLDFINCH

STATE FLOWER
WILD ROSE

The National Park Service has four sites in Iowa.

Deer are the largest wild animals that live in Iowa year round.

The Driftless Area National Wildlife Refuge is near McGregor. The Iowa Pleistocene snail is protected there. This tiny snail has existed for at least 400,000 years.

SOUTH DAKOTA

MINNESOTA

WISCONSIN

McGregor

Missouri Valley

NEBRASKA

Prairie City

ILLINOIS

Want to watch animals in their natural homes? Then explore DeSoto National Wildlife Refuge. It's in western Iowa near Missouri Valley.

In the fall, many **migrating** waterbirds pass through. That includes more than 12,000 snow geese! You'll also see deer in the refuge. In the summer, they're caring for newborn fawns.

Watch for cottontail rabbits, too. They hop through the brush and nibble plants. You may see a raccoon in a hollow log. Its furry little face has a black mask. And look out for opossums. They can hang from branches by their tails!

Thousands of snow geese can be seen in one day at DeSoto National Wildlife Refuge.

DOCTORING BIRDS IN DEDHAM

Birds can get hurt in many ways. That's why Saving Our **Avian** Resources was founded. It's called SOAR for short. This organization takes in injured birds. It gives them medical care. The birds stay until they're well. Then SOAR releases them into the wild again.

You can visit SOAR in Dedham. Walk through and meet the feathered patients. They may have a broken leg or wing. But they can heal safely here.

Most of SOAR's patients are raptors. Those are birds that hunt animals for food. They include hawks, owls, eagles, and falcons.

A SOAR worker cares for this bald eagle, which flew into a power line. The bird helps SOAR teach others about raptors.

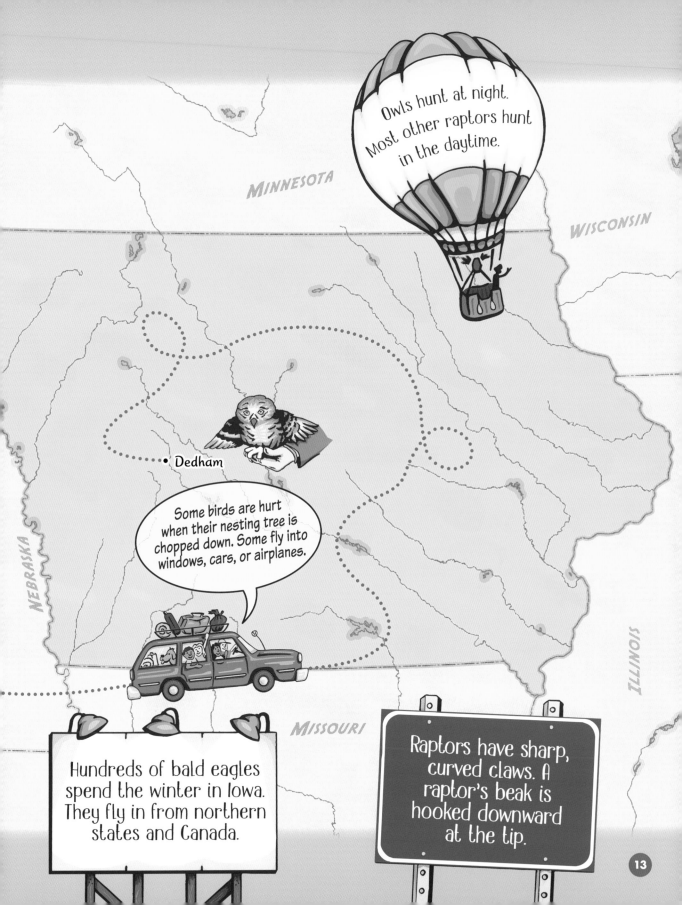

Owls hunt at night. Most other raptors hunt in the daytime.

Some birds are hurt when their nesting tree is chopped down. Some fly into windows, cars, or airplanes.

Hundreds of bald eagles spend the winter in Iowa. They fly in from northern states and Canada.

Raptors have sharp, curved claws. A raptor's beak is hooked downward at the tip.

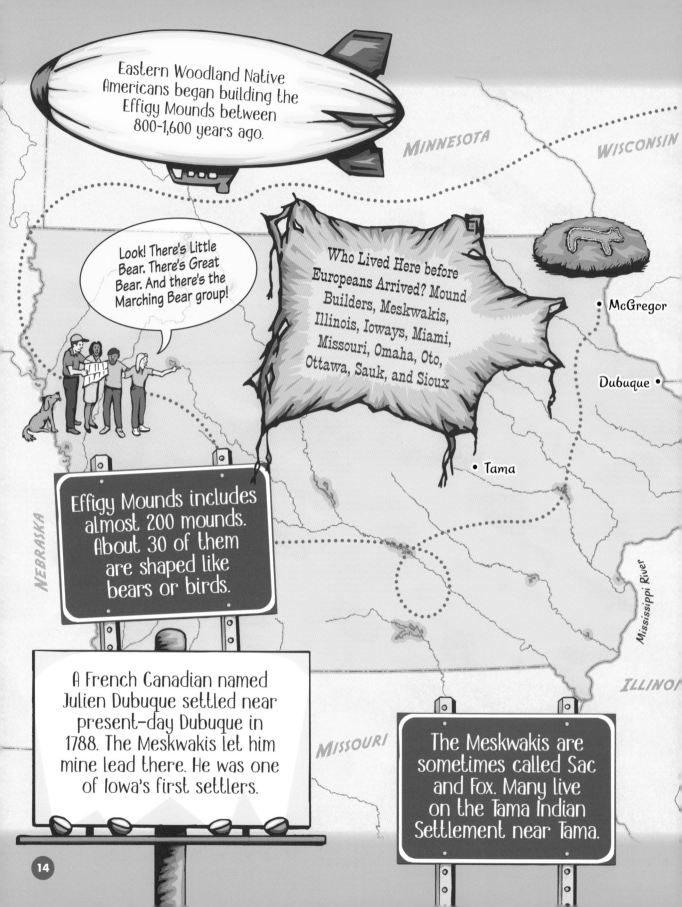

Eastern Woodland Native Americans began building the Effigy Mounds between 800-1,600 years ago.

Look! There's Little Bear. There's Great Bear. And there's the Marching Bear group!

Who Lived Here before Europeans Arrived? Mound Builders, Meskwakis, Illinois, Ioways, Miami, Missouri, Omaha, Oto, Ottawa, Sauk, and Sioux

MINNESOTA

WISCONSIN

• McGregor

Dubuque •

• Tama

Effigy Mounds includes almost 200 mounds. About 30 of them are shaped like bears or birds.

NEBRASKA

Mississippi River

ILLINOI

A French Canadian named Julien Dubuque settled near present-day Dubuque in 1788. The Meskwakis let him mine lead there. He was one of Iowa's first settlers.

MISSOURI

The Meskwakis are sometimes called Sac and Fox. Many live on the Tama Indian Settlement near Tama.

EFFIGY MOUNDS NATIONAL MONUMENT

First, you think you're seeing hills. But look a little closer. The hills form shapes and patterns. They're shaped like bears, birds, and other figures!

These hills are the **Effigy** Mounds near McGregor. Eastern Woodland Native Americans built them over hundreds of years. The mounds may have had religious purposes.

French explorers from Canada arrived in 1673. They were Louis Jolliet and Father Jacques Marquette. They came down the Mississippi River in canoes. Soon, fur traders moved into the region. They met several Native American groups. The Sauk and Meskwaki spent much of the year hunting and fishing. They moved throughout eastern Iowa and western Illinois. The Ioway also hunted, and they raised crops in the rich soil. They grew corn, sunflowers, and beans, among other crops.

Effigy Mounds is divided into four units. The Sny Magill Unit has the largest concentration of mounds.

Drop by the Sioux City Lewis and Clark Interpretive Center. Meriwether Lewis and William Clark led an expedition. They were going to the Pacific Ocean. Discover what life was like for the explorers as they traveled through the area that is now Sioux City. You'll learn about popular games the local Native Americans such as the Dakota played at the time. You'll also learn about Sergeant Charles Floyd. He was a member of the expedition.

Lewis and Clark passed along Iowa's western border in 1804. They reached the Pacific Ocean in 1805 and returned along Iowa's western border in 1806.

Lewis and Clark met with many Native Americans on their trip. They mapped rivers and studied animals, too. They built camps and forts for shelter.

This statue of Meriwether Lewis (right) and William Clark (left) stands outside the Lewis and Clark Interpretive Center.

MINNESOTA

WISCONSIN

Sioux City

Missouri River

NEBRASKA

ILLINOIS

Let's try to play one of these games! In *icaslohe econpi*, you roll a stone ball to try to knock down the other player's wood cylinder.

Sergeant Charles Floyd traveled with Lewis and Clark. He died on the trip and was buried on a bluff overlooking the Missouri River. The Sergeant Floyd Monument now stands at his burial site.

René-Robert Cavelier, sieur de La Salle, claimed a vast area for France in 1682. He named it Louisiana Territory. Iowa was part of this region. It passed to the United States in 1803.

Stand on the Crossroads compass at the Interpretive Center. The colors red, yellow, black, and white stand for the Native Americans who lived in Iowa before Lewis and Clark. The compass stands for the explorers and **immigrants** who came after Lewis and Clark.

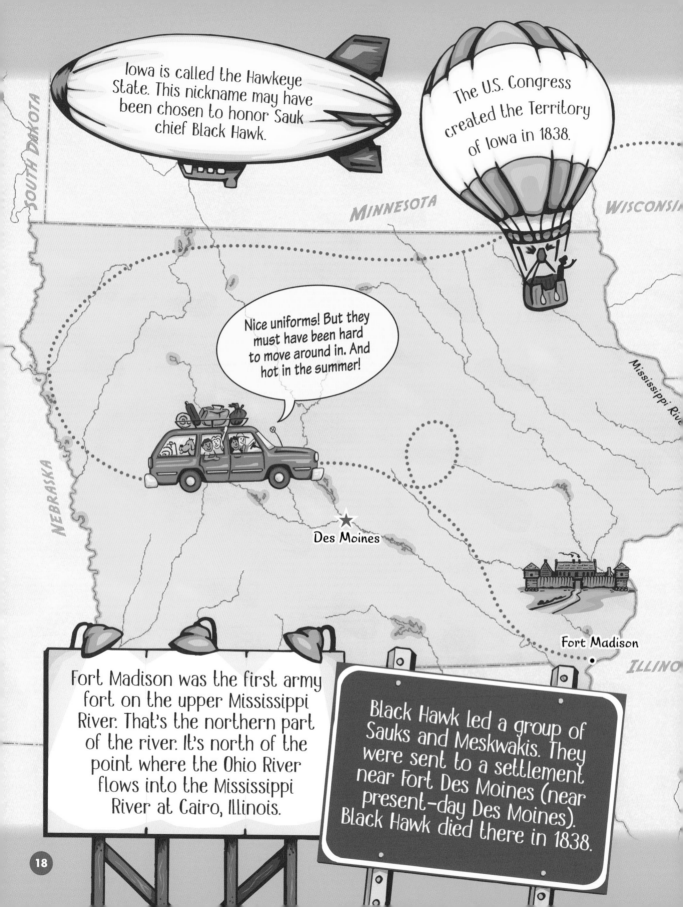

Wander through the log buildings. People in old-fashioned costumes dip candles or bake. Try lifting a heavy **musket**. You're visiting Old Fort Madison!

U.S. Army soldiers built Fort Madison in 1808. It protected a nearby fur-trading post. It sits just west of the Mississippi River.

The U.S. government began forcing Native Americans off their land in the 1800s. Sauk chief Black Hawk agreed to move in return for enough corn for the winter.

But the Sauks did not receive enough corn. So Black Hawk fought the U.S. army to keep his land in 1832. This is called the Black Hawk War. On August 2, 1832, the U.S. Army caught up with the Native Americans. They killed even the Native Americans who tried to surrender. The Sauks were forced onto a reservation in Iowa.

The United States Infantry used Old Fort Madison from 1808–1813.

THE AMANA COLONIES

See the old barns, bakeries, churches, and schools. Then browse through the shops. You'll see workers making furniture and woolen goods. You're at the Amana **Colonies**!

By the 1850s, settlers were pouring into Iowa. Many were immigrants. One group was the Amana Society. They left Germany seeking religious freedom. They founded their first Iowa village in 1855.

The Amana Society believed in sharing. All land and buildings belonged to the whole group. Each person had special tasks. They worked in kitchens, fields, or shops. Amana goods became known for their high quality.

The Amana colonists dug the Mill Race canal. The canal provided mills with waterpower.

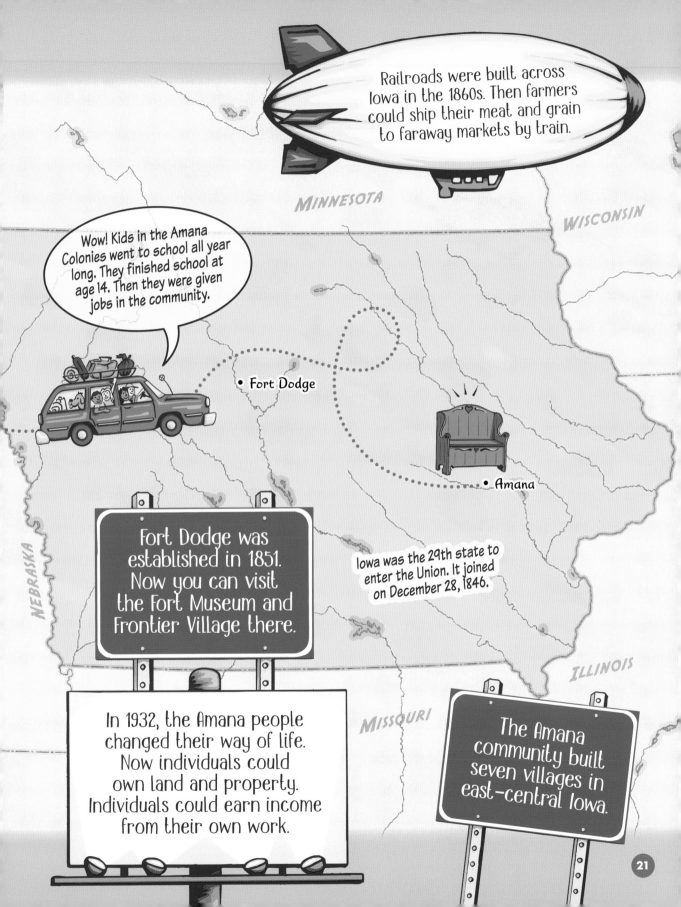

Railroads were built across Iowa in the 1860s. Then farmers could ship their meat and grain to faraway markets by train.

MINNESOTA

WISCONSIN

Wow! Kids in the Amana Colonies went to school all year long. They finished school at age 14. Then they were given jobs in the community.

• Fort Dodge

• Amana

NEBRASKA

Fort Dodge was established in 1851. Now you can visit the Fort Museum and Frontier Village there.

Iowa was the 29th state to enter the Union. It joined on December 28, 1846.

In 1932, the Amana people changed their way of life. Now individuals could own land and property. Individuals could earn income from their own work.

ILLINOIS

MISSOURI

The Amana community built seven villages in east-central Iowa.

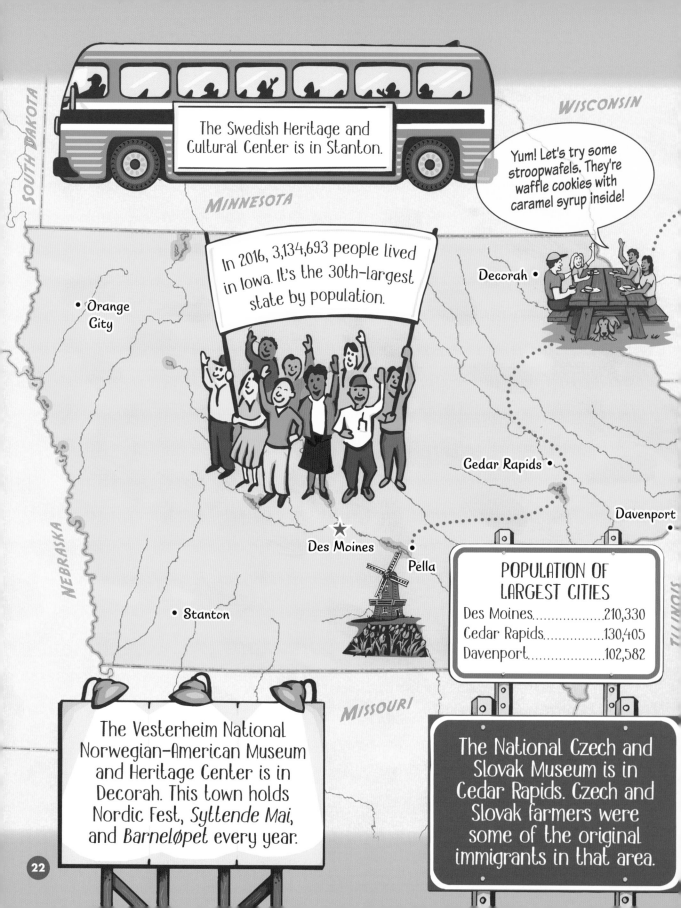

The Swedish Heritage and Cultural Center is in Stanton.

Yum! Let's try some stroopwafels. They're waffle cookies with caramel syrup inside!

In 2016, 3,134,693 people lived in Iowa. It's the 30th-largest state by population.

Decorah •

• Orange City

Cedar Rapids •

Davenport •

★
Des Moines

• Pella

• Stanton

POPULATION OF LARGEST CITIES
Des Moines.................210,330
Cedar Rapids..............130,405
Davenport..................102,582

The Vesterheim National Norwegian-American Museum and Heritage Center is in Decorah. This town holds Nordic Fest, *Syttende Mai*, and *Barneløpet* every year.

The National Czech and Slovak Museum is in Cedar Rapids. Czech and Slovak farmers were some of the original immigrants in that area.

SOUTH DAKOTA

MINNESOTA

WISCONSIN

NEBRASKA

MISSOURI

ILLINOIS

PELLA'S TULIP TIME FESTIVAL

Try some *vet bollen*. They're warm raisin doughnuts. Watch the dancers in their *klompen*. Those are **traditional** Dutch wooden shoes. Then look all around town. You see thousands of tulips in bloom. You're at the Pella Tulip Time Festival!

This festival celebrates Dutch **heritage**. Many Dutch immigrants settled around Pella. The Dutch are people from the Netherlands. This country is famous for growing tulips. So people in Pella planted tulips, too.

Many other immigrants came to Iowa. They all made new homes there. Many of these groups hold festivals today.

Both Pella and Orange City hold tulip festivals.

People dress in traditional Dutch costumes and play Dutch music at the Pella Tulip Time Festival.

How did Iowa life change over the years? Just visit the Living History Farms in Urbandale. You'll see communities from four periods in time. A tractor drops you off at the first farm!

Suppose you lived in Iowa about 1875. You might have visited towns such as Walnut Hill. It's built as a bustling frontier town. You'll see merchants and craftspeople there. They offered services for the region's farmers.

You'll also visit a farm from about 1900. Farmers had many machines by then. Some machines mowed hay or planted corn. Others tied crops into bundles. Horses pulled these machines along.

Learn how to make brooms at the Living History Farms!

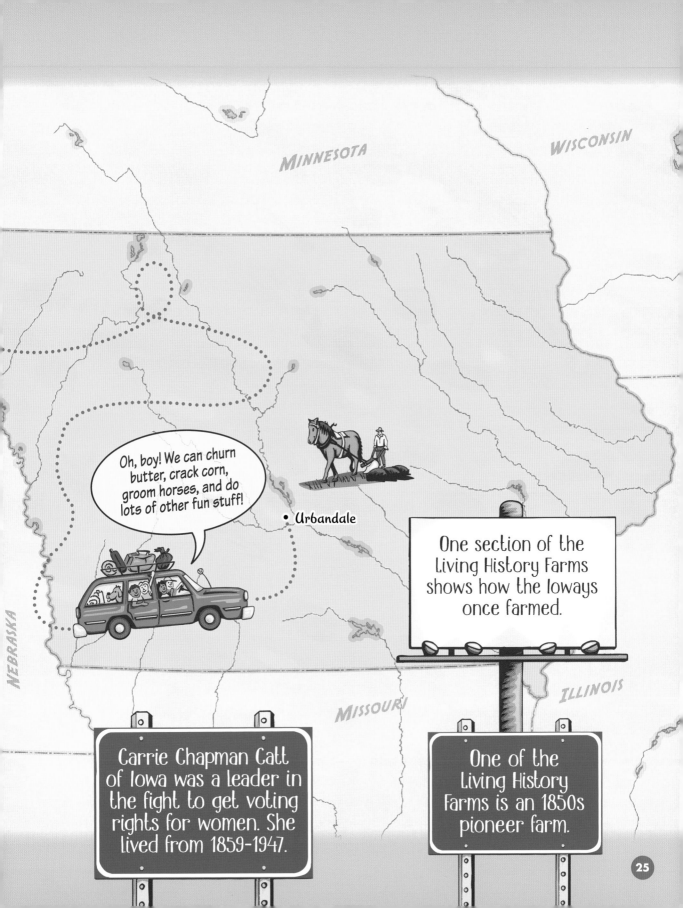

Iowa grows more corn than any other state.

Let's watch the tractor pull! Monster tractors pull a massive weight down a track. Whoever pulls it the farthest wins. If two tractors tie, they have a pull-off!

SOUTH DAKOTA

MINNESOTA

WISCONSIN

• Mason City

• Elgin

Many Iowa kids belong to 4-H clubs. Members work on projects related to farms and communities. The four Hs stand for head, heart, hands, and health.

• Atkins

★ • Mitchellville
Des Moines

The state fair is held in Des Moines in August each year.

NEBRASKA

ILLINOIS

MISSOURI

Elgin, Mitchellville, and Atkins have maize mazes. Maize is another name for corn. And a maze is a confusing arrangement of paths. You wander between the corn rows and try to find your way out!

What Does Iowa Raise?
Corn, hogs, soybeans, and beef cattle

MASON CITY'S NORTH IOWA FAIR

See who wins the tallest-cornstalk contest. Check out a horse show. Or watch dogs show off obedience skills. Then catch the hog show. You won't believe how big hogs can grow!

You're enjoying Mason City's North Iowa Fair. Many Iowa cities hold farm fairs. The biggest fair is the Iowa State Fair. It's held in Des Moines every year.

Farms cover most of Iowa. Corn is the state's leading crop. Soybeans are an important crop, too.

What becomes of the corn and soybeans? Hogs and cattle eat a lot of these crops. Iowa raises more hogs than any other state!

Meet baby pigs at the Iowa State Fair!

THE JOHN DEERE TRACTOR FACTORY IN WATERLOO

Make sure you're wearing closed-toed shoes. Your toes might not be safe in sandals. Then hop on the tour cart. It's pulled by a John Deere tractor! You'll zoom all over the John Deere Tractor Factory. There you'll see how big, green tractors are made!

Farm machinery is an important Iowa product. Some factories make construction machinery, too. But foods are Iowa's top factory goods. Some food plants process and package meat. They might make hogs into ham or sausage. Other food plants process crops. Take corn, for example. It's made into corn oil or cornmeal. And don't forget another great corn product—popcorn!

Don't forget to stop by the John Deere Tractor and Engine Museum while you are in Waterloo!

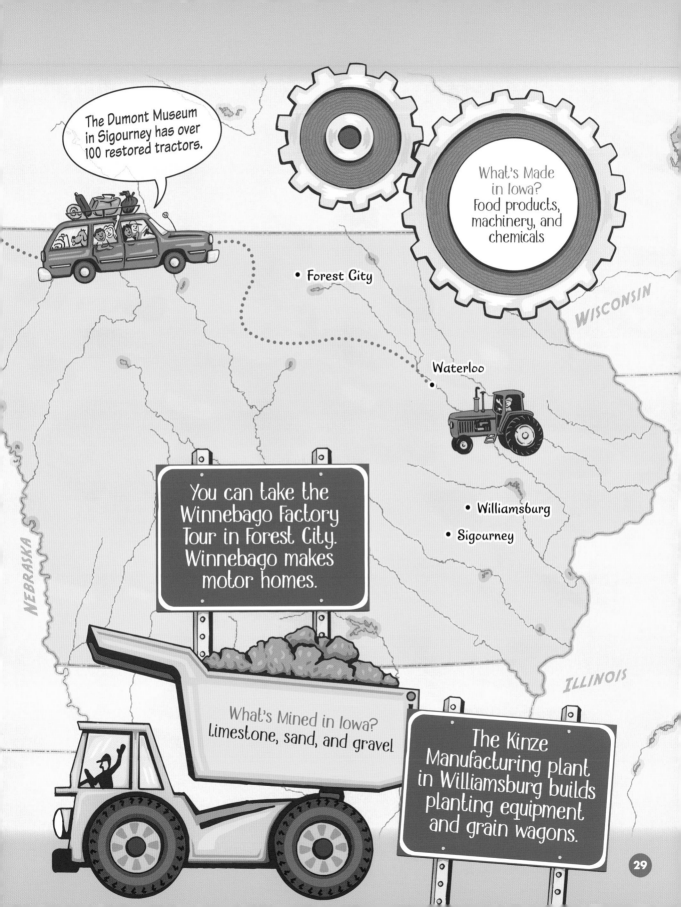

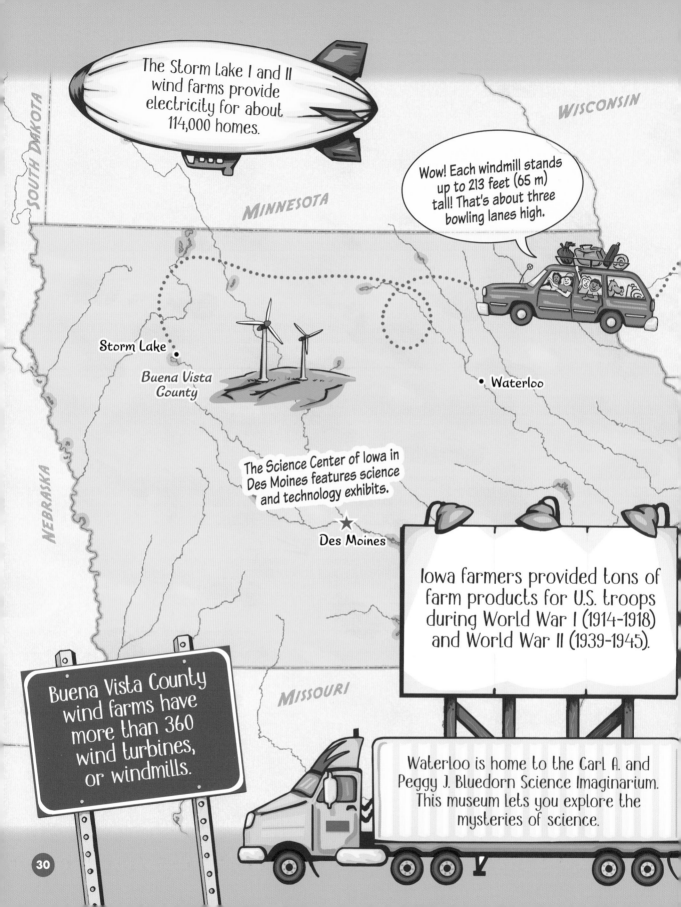

BUENA VISTA COUNTY WIND FARMS

Head out to Buffalo Ridge near Storm Lake. You'll see rows of huge, three-armed windmills. You've found a Buena Vista County wind farm!

In the 1900s, Iowans looked toward the future. They saw that the country faced energy problems. Oil, gas, and coal are common energy sources. But they release harmful materials into the **environment**. These sources won't last forever, either. And when supplies are low, energy prices soar.

Some Iowans decided to create electricity with wind power. Wind is clean, and it doesn't run out. Wind turns the wind farm's windmills. And that creates electricity for thousands of homes.

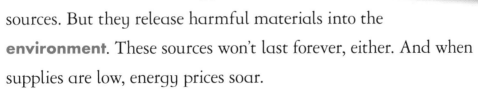

Wind farms can be found all over Iowa.

THE STATE CAPITOL IN DES MOINES

Y ou'll know when you're in Des Moines. Just look across the skyline. You'll see something golden glistening in the sun. It's the state capitol's big, rounded dome!

Inside this grand building are state government offices. Iowa has three branches of government. One branch makes the state's laws. Its members belong to Iowa's General Assembly. The governor heads another branch. It enforces, or carries out, the laws. The third branch is made up of judges. They apply the laws. That means they listen to cases in courts. Then they decide if someone has broken the law.

Keep an eye out for the glass floor in the Capitol!

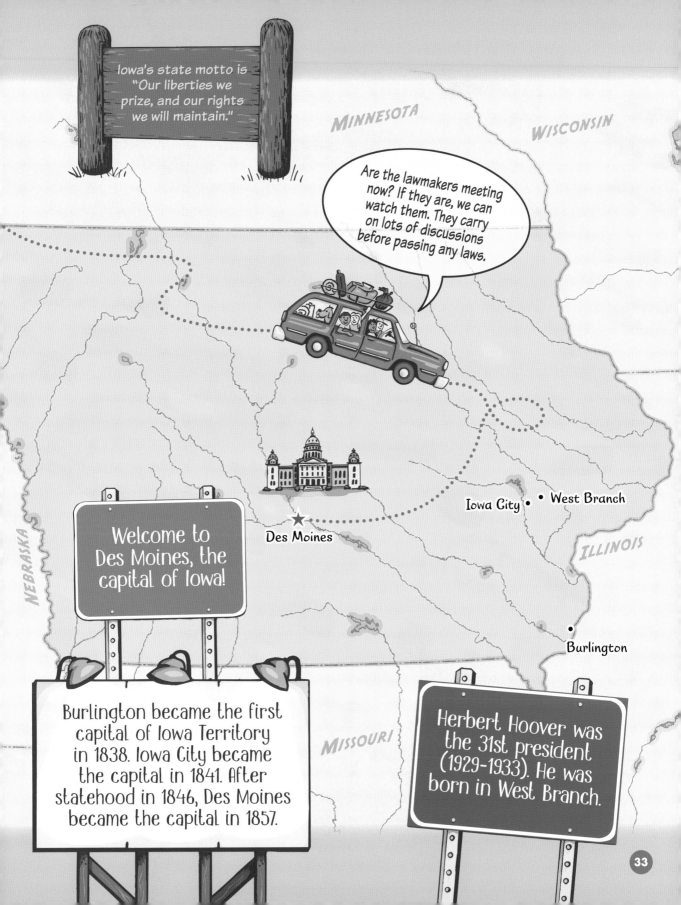

Iowa's state motto is "Our liberties we prize, and our rights we will maintain."

Are the lawmakers meeting now? If they are, we can watch them. They carry on lots of discussions before passing any laws.

Welcome to Des Moines, the capital of Iowa!

Des Moines

Iowa City • • West Branch

Burlington

Burlington became the first capital of Iowa Territory in 1838. Iowa City became the capital in 1841. After statehood in 1846, Des Moines became the capital in 1857.

Herbert Hoover was the 31st president (1929-1933). He was born in West Branch.

THE ICE CREAM CAPITAL OF THE WORLD

Do you like ice cream? Then visit the Blue Bunny Ice Cream Parlor in Le Mars. They have more than 40 flavors of ice cream!

Blue Bunny is owned by Wells Enterprises. They make their ice cream in Le Mars. No spot in the world makes more ice cream.

Iowa's General Assembly decided to honor Le Mars. It gave the city a delicious-sounding nickname. Can you guess what that nickname is? The Ice Cream Capital of the World!

Drop by the gift shop when you finish your ice cream. You can buy Blue Bunny ice cream bowls and tumblers!

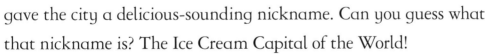

Not in the mood for a cone? Try one of the Ice Cream Parlor's shakes!

OUR TRIP

We visited many amazing places on our trip! We also met a lot of interesting people along the way. Look at the map below. Use your finger to trace all the places we have been.

When did Iowa's first public library open? *See page 9 for the answer.*

Which Iowa animal is a marsupial? *Page 10 has the answer.*

When do owls hunt? *See page 13 for the answer.*

When were the Effigy Mounds built? *Look on page 14 for the answer.*

How many villages did the Amana community build? *Page 21 has the answer.*

Who was Carrie Chapman Catt? *Turn to page 25 for the answer.*

What crop does Iowa grow more of than any other state? *Look on page 26 for the answer.*

How many homes are powered by the Storm Lake wind farms? *Look o Turn to page 30 for the answer.*

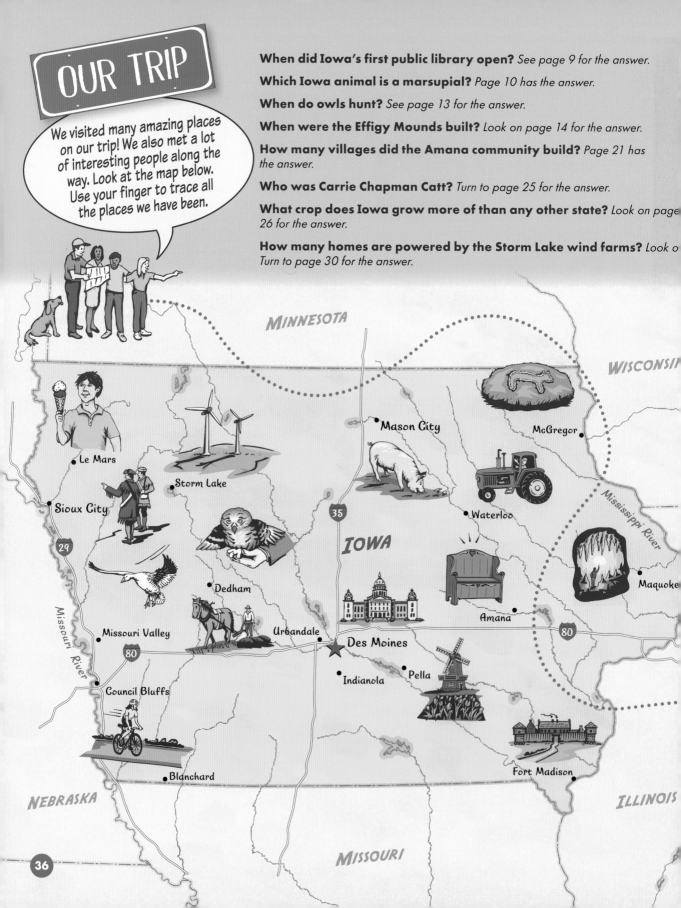

MINNESOTA

WISCONSIN

Le Mars

Storm Lake

Sioux City

Mason City

McGregor

Mississippi River

Waterloo

IOWA

Maquoke

Dedham

Amana

Missouri Valley

Des Moines

Urbandale

Council Bluffs

Indianola

Pella

Missouri River

Blanchard

Fort Madison

NEBRASKA

ILLINOIS

MISSOURI

State flag

State seal

That was a great trip! We have traveled all over Iowa! There are a few places that we didn't have time for, though. Next time, we plan to visit the National Balloon Classic in Indianola. Visitors can ride in a hot-air balloon.

STATE SYMBOLS

State bird: Eastern goldfinch (wild canary)
State flower: Wild rose
State rock: Geode
State tree: Oak

STATE SONG

"SONG OF IOWA"

Words by S. H. M. Byers, sung to the tune of the traditional Christmas song "O Tannenbaum"

You asked what land I love the best,
Iowa, 'tis Iowa,
The fairest State of all the west, Iowa,
O! Iowa.
From yonder Mississippi's stream
To where Missouri's waters gleam
O! fair it is as poet's dream, Iowa,
in Iowa.

See yonder fields of tasseled corn, Iowa,
in Iowa,
Where plenty fills her golden horn, Iowa,
in Iowa.
See how her wondrous prairies shine
To yonder sunset's purpling line.
O! Happy land, O! land of mine, Iowa,
O! Iowa.

And she has maids whose laughing eyes,
Iowa, O! Iowa.
To him whose loves were Paradise, Iowa,
O! Iowa.
O! happiest fate that e'er was known.
Such eyes to shine for one alone,
To call such beauty all his own. Iowa,
O! Iowa.

Go read the story of thy past, Iowa, O!
Iowa.
What glorious deeds, what fame thou
hast! Iowa, O! Iowa.
So long as time's great cycle runs,
Or nations weep their fallen ones,
Thou'lt not forget thy patriot sons, Iowa,
O! Iowa.

FAMOUS PEOPLE

Black Hawk (1767–1838), Sauk leader who lived in Iowa

Carothers, Wallace Hume (1896–1937), chemist and inventor

Carson, Johnny (1925–2005), talk show host

Cody, William Frederick "Buffalo Bill" (1846–1917), scout and showman

Gallup, George H. (1901–1984), pollster

Glaspell, Susan (1876–1948), author

Hoover, Herbert (1874–1964), 31st U.S. president

Johnson, Shawn (1992–), gymnast

Kutcher, Ashton (1987–), actor

Lopez, Cody "Seth Rollins" (1986–), wrestler

Miller, Glenn (1904–1944), bandleader

Ruess, Nate (1982–), singer and songwriter

Sproles, Darren (1983–), football player

Sunday, Billy (1862–1935), baseball player and evangelist

Wacha, Michael (1991–), baseball player

Warner, Kurt (1971–), former football player

Wayne, John (1907–1979), actor

Williams, Andy (1927–2012), singer

Wood, Elijah (1981–), actor

Wood, Grant (1891–1942), painter

WORDS TO KNOW

avian (AY-vee-uhn) relating to birds

bluffs (BLUHFS) high, steep banks

colonies (KOL-uh-neez) settlements that often have ties with a mother country

effigy (EF-uh-gee) an image or model of a person or animal

environment (en-VYE-ruhn-muhnt) natural surroundings such as air, water, and soil

heritage (HARE-uh-tij) the customs passed on by a group of people over the years

immigrants (IM-uh-gruhnts) people who move to another country

migrating (MYE-grate-ing) traveling to another location as the seasons change

musket (MUHSS-kit) an early type of rifle

prairies (PRAIR-eez) flat or gently rolling lands covered by grasses

traditional (truh-DISH-uhn-uhl) following long-held customs

TO LEARN MORE

IN THE LIBRARY

St. George, Judith. *What Was the Lewis and Clark Expedition?* New York, NY: Grosset & Dunlap, 2014.

Winans, Jay D. *Iowa: The Hawkeye State.* New York, NY: AV2 by Weigl, 2016.

ON THE WEB
Visit our Web site for links about Iowa:
childsworld.com/links

Note to Parents, Teachers, and Librarians: We routinely verify our Web links to make sure they are safe and active sites. So encourage your readers to check them out!

PLACES TO VISIT OR CONTACT
Iowa Tourism Office

traveliowa.com
200 East Grand Avenue
Des Moines, IA 50309
800/345-4692
For more information about traveling in Iowa

State Historical Society of Iowa
iowaculture.gov/history
600 East Locust Street
Des Moines, IA 50319
515/281-5111
For more information about the history of Iowa

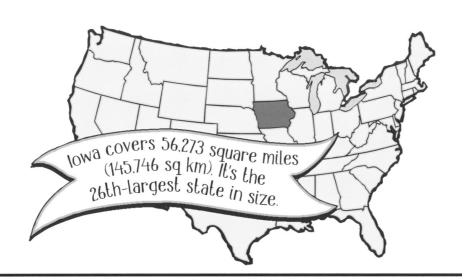

Iowa covers 56,273 square miles (145,746 sq km). It's the 26th-largest state in size.

INDEX

Bye, Hawkeye State. We had a great time. We'll come back soon!